HEART SNITCHED

~KIRTHANA SASTRY

I took the risk and

Let my heart snitch

Contents

House on fire   6

Past Imperfect   20

Soft thick skin   46

A little uncomfortable aches   72

House on fire

My ears absorb the poison as you speak
Am I even human if I don't fall for your filthy lies
What started as a hello
Has now become I can't stand your existence
anymore
Cheated on my mind
To reopen the doors of my heart to you
I think I was not satisfied by the pain you
caused last time
And now here you are again with your
charming lies
   "Welcome back to the home you broke
    I hope your stay is not long" I say
Now I have become a little wiser than before
(hopefully)
Trying to master the art of not getting trapped
Into your web of lies

They think covering their ears
Will help them ignore the bombardment
The chaos flowed into the eardrums
Igniting fights between the family
Who is vulnerable and who is not
All are soaking in the *tragedy*

Words as sharp as knives and daggers
Are thrown at each other
Soon the violence becomes silent
Slowly they lumber
Feeling guilty for their sins
It's too late for an apology
As comfort slips off their skins

~failed efforts for lost happiness

Hello world
Wait! You are not on fire?
Or did I assume you were burning into flames?
Just because I came from a house constantly
on fire
I thought love was not worthwhile
Being cold-hearted is a habit
Back-stabbing people with cruelty is common
Hiding the struggles is called being brave
I was wrong as I walked in the open
Hiding my scares
Thinking that everyone around me
Only feel the pain and have not found peace
Just like me
But I don't see ashes around me
Nor do I inhale the burning air
I hear birds chirping and flowers blooming
I did not feel congested anymore
Which is such a contrary statement to say
As I was walking in the fire all this long

I knocked on many doors
Trying to occupy spaces
Which my soul can call home

You gave me the pain I did not deserve
Also showered me with the love I longed for
I'm still in denial
That my heart *wants you* around

Living in the same four walls
But I am not ready to *suffer the guilt*

To be away from you either

~stuck in an endless loop

How can I stop daydreaming
About living a life free from brutality
A life in which my mother
Does not sleep with a tear-stained face
Living in a web of lies and loud cries
A life in which my father
Listens to my heart
Showers me with love
Acknowledges me for me
A life where I don't have the
Regret to see a new morning
But is this going to be a reality
Or am I just wasting my wishes?

You cause all the pain
And call it a day
Leaving behind your ugly stains
My heart is not tame
Until I take revenge
I feel there is no shame
Feeding you the same pain
There is no need to justify revenge
As for my soul
It is the only way to quench

~family arguments

Trying to hold back tears
Because they said
        "Only cowards cry"
Trying not to show overwhelming happiness
Because they said
        "Dont act crazy"
Trying to hide the scars
Because they said
        "You are a failure
I did everything they said
Then why do I still feel caged?

Congestion in my heart
A room full of people
An urge to scream
Words that are evil
Questioning my own sanity
I'm stuck in the web of brutality
Suppressed emotions
I feel that I am a step away from an explosion

Grief became the fulcrum
That held us together
We became good
At consoling ourselves
For the foul play
We committed with our ugly minds
Hell was the distance between us
We bled shades of grief
Shades of pain
Shades of envy
More than the shades of joy
Did we deserve what conspired
Or is this the way to move forward in life?

Past Imperfect

The current situation in which we stand in
Would not have transpired
If we had fixed all the missing pieces
And made peace

~carrying past ruins

I am not where I want to be
I am trying to fill a void
Shedding tears
Tearing myself apart
Only to satisfy other's ego
"Is god listening to my prayers?"
        I yell at my mother
Now even the thought of the future
Is giving me a scare
Feels like I'm reliving the traumas of yesterday
Again and again
It's exhausting me
Helpless and alone
I am my own savior
But for how long?

I gave a lot of time
To people who poured poison
With actions and words
Trying to tag along with their actions
I gave them complete control of me
I feared to be left out
Trying to avoid being pulled into the dark space
A prey to manipulation
A miserable soul filled with frustration
Is what I had become
Circled in the same path of *pretended love*

Now I can mimic the act to be completely *alive*

When everything inside me is *dead*

~self decay

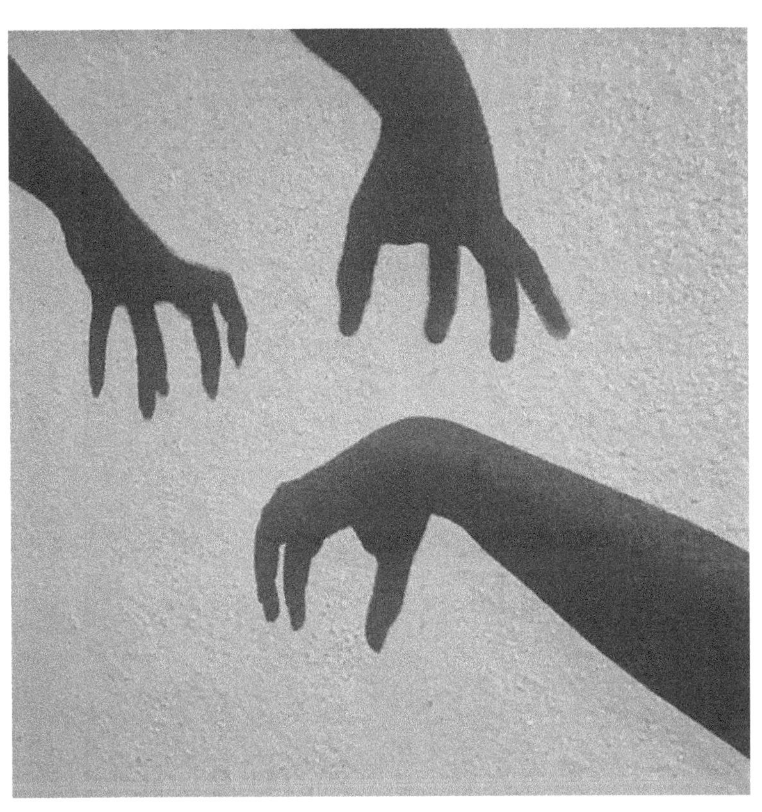

Yesterday I was honest with myself
Trying to extract the reasons for my hurting
Starring at the fresh scars
I feel I'm stuck in the loop of regret and pain
Constantly harming the body
Maybe it was better to continue the suffering
Because yesterday I was honest with myself
And today I am completely lonely

How long does rage last?
A few seconds or a few days?
The regrets of the past
Accumulating in my veins
The very little love that remained
Started to fade
The act of normalization
Cutting deeper than a blade
All this effort to fake a smile
Is it really worthwhile?
I didn't find my path to escape
My body was covered in caution tape
As my actions bared concequences
Showing rage became a comfort
Silent cries turned into thunderous screams
Every day felt like adding new bits of pain
To the incomplete past
I think it was ok to live like this

Every time I absorb
The vicious words thrown at me
A piece of me goes missing
Succumbing to the evil minds
Over the years I have become a puzzle
Did I not realize
I was running in a loop over and over
Until the whole of me went missing
And all that was left was a hallow heart

Did you find the peace you always wanted
When you threw me out of your life
Or did my absence leave you in a void?

I'm cleaning out the mess
That was left behind from yesterday's storm
Ruins of me scattered everywhere
Picking it up bit by bit
Molding it into something new
Just for me to be ruined again
By even a mightier storm
On a different day
By a different person

I don't have a beautiful past
The one that's filled with infinite happy
memories
I never dared to change my present
As I got used to Life that was unpleasant
The hope for a happy ending rests in my mind
But will it ever end well when
All I have carried from my past is
Painful scars and chaotic traumas?

If you have survived this long
Then you have dodged many bullets
Shot from loud and unwanted mouths
Take a bow
Because it is never easy
To ignore the harsh remarks
It is never a shame to show your scars
Even being a mess can be beautiful
With grace, you have come this far
Maybe now is the time to live
The war has been fought
You stood like a rock
Shielding yourself from the bullets
Let your heart rest

I screamed loud and clear
Didn't you hear?
I wanted you to loosen your grip
Now your fingerprints rest on my hand
Did you not notice my heart rip?
Or was my forced smile persuasive?
I tried to forget and forgive
But your actions left a dent
Making me lose a reason to live

Don't you blame yourself for those wounds?
You asked
I realized that these wounds
I carried from my past
Is the main reason I have learned to respect
myself
And take time to heal

The ghosts of the past still haunt me
The image of them burns my head
Mostly similar faces
Who promised never to break me apart
But now I have lost their traces
The weight of their memory
Is painful in my heart
Midnights have become dreadful
Cause these memories are tearing me apart
I wish to leave the past behind
But it's clinging like the brown leaves
During autumn weather
Dead and sad

Buried deep under the hope
Of forever lasting smiles
My emotions hanging at the edge of the rope
I waited for time to heal me
Assembling barricades in my surroundings
I wanted to feel free
But hate came through
Shattering what had healed
And made me bleed
I feel like a grey cloud
Even on the brightest summer days
Soaking up the remains of foul plays
I made the mistake of hoping
Hoping I can gain the smile back
But now the will to survive is what I lack

Pulling tricks of manipulation from the hat
It was all glitter and shine
I saw it with wide-open eyes
One trick after the other
My mind is eating all your lies
Like it was starving all this while
    "I will never break your heart"
        You said
It was one of your first tricks on me
It's funny how you took everything from me
The tenderness and the happiness
And I am still here being your pray
It all feels like a magic show
Where I am that one lucky girl in the audience
Who do you select to perform the magic on

They say they have carved a path
They ask me to follow it
They make me assume that
There is a future as bright as the sun
At the end of it
I am walking down the path now
It's not smooth or filled with flowers and
butterflies
I look back
Total darkness and *Voices of failure* echoing

I ask myself
Is this really the path I want to take?
What if it does not lead me to the *life I want to
lead*?

If I turn back
Will it be considered as my *defeat*?

My brain and heart are not in phase
The brain tries so hard to catch up
But the heart is always ahead of portraying
reflexes
That has hurtful consequences
The heart snitched way too loud
The body was not in sync
It all happened in a second
Undigestable for the brain
Thinking of several ways to undo what's done
It asks me whether it is a better option to die
Rather then talk

Rip to all those
Who has been buried
Somewhere deep in my heart
Where I can't find them
Now I am on a hunt
To find someone new
Who will break me completely
So I can dig a new grave

                         ~habits

So I finally decided to let you in my heart
But you decided to pry into my past
Foolish mind thought it would be nice
To have a new visitor
But little did it know
That you will leave dirty footprints
All over the heart
You had planned your scheme of betrayal
And I fell right into it
You left me with love unstable
And traumas that are several
Now your memories are a part of me
I can't get rid of it even if I try

I poured love on everyone in the room
In return I was served a platter of betrayal
I miss read the room
Now I have learned to gulp down chaos
Like water

We reap what we sow
Narrated often
We are the victims of our actions
Getting accustomed to the patterns
Of the daily routines we create
          If there is ever a slight glitch in
the pattern
          We lose ourselves completely
          Bonding with loneliness
Its the impact
Our actions have made us
The impact grows like creepers
An urge to undo it all
But the damage caused is long-lasting
And now we forever remain the victims

After all, you are the victim here
You sucked every bit of good in me
Leaving me gray
Your intentions are never clear
Or maybe I'm just blind
Leave me alone to scream
In the chaos you have created
I'm the one bearing the consequences of your actions
You still blame me for pointing a finger
Because after all
you are the Victim here

Soft thick skin

Today I learned to dance with flames
Matching my steps with the tunes of fire
I don't feel the heat
I'm just here in the middle of it
While you pour the fuel
Feeding the fire
I thought I would end up in ashes initially
But as the flames grew
My skin grew thicker
Shielding my fragile heart

We grew up ignoring the warnings
Given to us by elders
We failed to develop a thick skin
Towards what the society
Is throwing at us today
Society will make you cry
And ask why are you so fragile
It will make you despise
Your beautiful body
And tell you to stop starving yourself
Completely dead inside
You master how to fake a smile
Because shedding tears makes you weak
Walking forward with a dozen swords
Stabbed on your back by the society
Makes you strong
You ask yourself which face
You are choosing to wear today
To stand in front of the society
Consider yourself a pray
Because it is too late to escape

I lost my consciousness
When I drowned in the sea of lies
I laughed at the depth
Misunderstanding it to be shallow
The lies pull me down
The heavyweight on my body
My lungs could not take it
I go down deep enough
Where no one could ever save me

I have inhaled so much agony
My heart and the feeling of contentment
Hiss at each other

What sabotaging fragile existence looks like
Painful?
Cruel?
There is plenty of air
I'm still gasping to breath
I was not ready for this war
Yet the pain is absorbed into my skin
Just like water crawling into the roots
If there was only an option to refute
I wouldn't have to fake laughter
So now I know why caged birds sing

The most melodious tunes

I should have defined constructive criticism a
little better
My voice crakes a little while I narrate a poem
The same poem I wrote down spending hours
Trying all the words that rhyme with happy,
flowers, and more
Just to make it more worth
So you can shower a little appreciation
Maybe tell me that I am great
But not the opposite of it

~seeking validation

I am created in a way
Where the catastrophe of my actions
Shines brighter than my character
Words come out of my mouth unfiltered
Leaving me uncontrollable
Will I ever find someone who adores my
catastrophe?
Someone who makes peace with chaos

You are not having a panic attack, you will be
fine
Are you sure?
Cause my heart is racing so fast
I can almost feel it reaching my throat
I want to shout my brains out
Cause I can't keep the pain in anymore
My hands have become involuntary
Making me tear my skin out
Bloods boiling inside my veins
Tears are staining my face
Running down my neck
Are these reactions common
For someone who has been tortured by a
sadist
Will I be fine when I have been completely
ripped apart?

~An episode

Healing is:

Shedding many layers of worn out flesh

Doing *poetic justice* to trauma

Throwing away *tear stained* pillows

Making an effort to *forget* and *forgive*

Many brutal wars have been fought
To become this soft
A lot of god's given light
Has been used to heal other broken hearts
Turned into water
Unafraid to touch open wounds
Not expecting the same favor in return
But a small beg to not be scared
While I mend yours

The inside of me is a whole new person
The skin visible to the outside world
Resembles that of a chameleon
Changing according to how people want to see me
Not so stubborn
Not so bold
Not very happy
Completely under compulsion
The person inside me laughs looking at what I have become
In the eyes of the audience
Almost like a rag doll tossed everywhere
Covered in dust and stains

Tolerance and I do not get along
It has always been a strange relationship
I am scared when the anger emerges out
Dont mistake it to be subtle
You might choke

~save yourself from trouble

Imprints left on my soul
I have changed into so many shapes
Shredded a lot of soft thick skin
During the process of molding myself
I wanted to know what the future looks like
I held on to hope between my fingers
Trying hard not to let them slip
Hopes for a future as bright as a garden full of
flowers

I try to trap my innocence
In the web of cruelty
Like it is a recompense
For all the pain I have suffered
The wounds are covered
The mouth has been stitched shut
As I want to take pride
Into showing the world
That I have mastered the art of developing a
thick skin

~took a bow for bravery

Observing the *miracles* created by the inner
child inside me
Is the favorite chor of the adult me

The earth smiles through flowers
Clouds cry through the rain
Sun screams through the humid heat
When nature has the freedom to express
Why do we stitch our mouths tight
When we are given the chance
To point out why we are hurting

In my head
I am always right
The consequences of my actions
The power my words hold
Are always right

It is just my way of surviving
From the sharp teeth of society
Preventing my softness to become pray

Standing up for myself
Thinking I am brave
How did I not realize
That I was digging my own grave
When I decided to be me
Do things that my heart told me too
I was told that my actions were wrong
"This is the wrong way of leading your life"
    They mocked simultaneously
Life felt like a movie scene
Where I was a one-women army
Trying hard to shield myself from
everyone who tried hard to pull me down

A message to the inner child inside me

Hi, it's me years later trying to connect with you
I know I have failed to become the person
You have always dreamed of
Ignored all your desperate cries
Where was I you ask?
I was lost in doing
What the world wanted me to do
Sabotaging my happiness for theirs
Trying hard to fit into spaces
Where I did not belong
Gave underserved people a second chance
But please don't you give up on me
As I'm trying to heal us
I don't blame you for what's happened
I am learning to see the world through your
eyes

A little uncomfortable aches

I set myself free from your approval
Shower me with your disgust
I have learned to co-exist
My emotions are covered with rust
They waited too long to be heard
You turned a deaf year to my screams
It is ok if hate fills your body at the glance of
me
As I feel myself now more than ever
Not pretending to be someone else
For your love

Choose your excuses wisely
To not let people disguised as knives
Enter the red carpet into your life
An escape from them
Will prevent bruises disguised as words
From hurting your frail heart
This way of learning to escape is called
surviving
To survive is to protect yourself
Your body is the only place
You have to lodge
Never let the heart choose
The people who enter
Some might be backstabbers in disguise
Hard to identify
You are slowly absorbed into their darkness
Bruise after bruise forms on the flesh
A rag doll you will become
So never give your mind a chance to scream
An excuse then would have prevented
Many painful screams and long-lasting scars

~Gatted heart

A part of me wants to take the risk
It may or may not be worth it
The other part is afraid
Of the ugly glances and talks
Running between these places
A little guilt I swallow
What if everything changes?
Will my achievements be looked down
Or the talk of the town

I burst out laughing hearing a joke
I felt it to be so funny that I laughed until my
stomach hurt
Soon tears started rolling out of my eyes
Tears of joy
                    "You never looked this happy in
a while"
Because you have brought my happiness back
Which was once stolen
My heart feels whole

Today I had a public breakdown
Tears falling through the spaces between my
fingers
When I tried to hide my face from everyone's
view
Strangers came to comfort me like
Like they knew the reason
It's not common to see someone cry in public I
guess (laughs)
People might think that I am an
attention-seeker
But my tears could not hold back
As my emotions pushed them off the cliff
Too ashamed and helpless
I feel like I have shown my weakness so bright
Only a switch back in time can help me

With open arms society welcomed chaos
Encouraged it to outstay its duration
Burned down the love persisting
Between the beloved ones
Until the hearts rusted

Society makes people triumph in chaos
Teaches them that this is the way
Life should be lead
Over time chaos becomes a comfort
Making you a part of the society
Now you are one of them
Because chaos is the reason
You smile

~Now I am society

You looked at the scars on my hand
Ran your fingers on them
Like you have the magic to heal
But how can you not realize
That behind the pain
you are the main reason
Disguised as the demon
Trying to pour poison
Into my head
Now your actions are something I dread

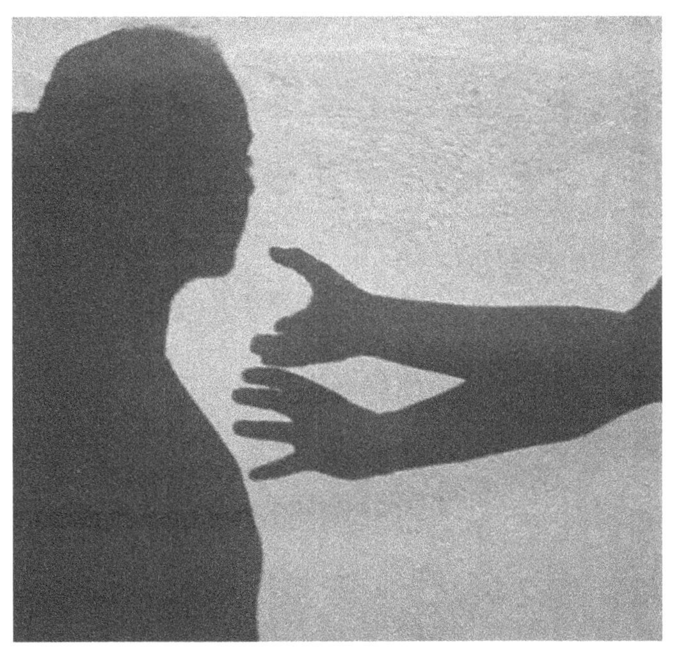

My heart is a wildflower
Withstanding all the storms
Standing tall and strong
It has healed between the cracks
Of broken places
Not surrendering to the horror
I hope to show it the bluest sky one day
So it can grow as a warrior

My body is a volcano
Anger and lava are the same no?
I keep quiet for a while
Trying to calm the boiling blood
Unable to figure out
What triggered
Was it their actions?
Or was it my naiveness?
I burst out at times
With frustration at it's peak
Rues and pain covering my skin
In the same way
Fragments of rocks and lava
Flowing through the vents
Covering the surface of the earth
It is never the end
But has become a monthly chore

My demons are my companions
Walking beside me
Shadowing my next move
Before they used to haunt my dreams
Now they come in all types of bodies and sizes
Haunting me in real life
A constant reason to my heart aches
Something I can't get rid of
I have come this far bearing them
It is strange cause they started to feel
A little like long lost soulmates

~Turned a blind eye

I thought I felt that spark
A little bit of love and laughter we shared
But I did not know that I would be left alone in
the dark
Taping bandages on a broken future
Just because I caught a temporary feeling
I was gullible
So you started peeling
My skin little by little
Until I lost hope of chasing the brightness
again

You are rotting from the inside
		Really?
			How can you tell?
The brightest smile in the room
Is now a dark frown
The once always cheerful talks
Has now turned gloomy
Cracks of heartbreak appear in your voice
Like you are constantly in war
Lost poise
Absorbed pain like a sponge
It's true that the sensitive suffers more
Look at you
Gradually getting destroyed
Just like rotten plants
Loosing all their bright greenness
Taking away the essence from the room

Fright runs down the spine
I shudder when your finger touches my skin
During days of bright sunshine
I feel I'm under pouring rain
When my eyes see the evilness in yours
It is hard to stop myself from going sane
My heart is in my throat
Fingers tremble and feet are frozen
Only suffering is what I wrote
Are you just a phase
Or you are here to stay
I was not warned of your arrival
But now I'm begging for my survival

~rain during summer

Welcome to the process of growth
Where it is okay for heartaches to pain
Scars to run down your skin
Tears to stain your cheeks
Emotions to churn inside your stomach
Your old soul will forgive you
It has undergone several phases of growth
Just like yours
It lights a small spark in your heart
To keep you growing
There might be the worst weather
Acting as a hindrance
Forcing you to give up
But just like the prettiest flowers
You will bloom